D0972992

Angélique

Angélique

Lorena Gale

Playwrights Canada Press
Toronto

PLAYWRIGHTS CANADA PRESS
The Canadian Drama Publisher
215 Spadina Ave., Suite 230, Toronto, Ontario, Canada, M5T 2C7
phone 416.703.0013   fax 416.408.3402
orders@playwrightscanada.com • www.playwrightscanada.com

Playwrights Canada Press acknowledges the financial support of the Government of
Canada through the Canada Book Fund and the Canada Council for the Arts and the
Province of Ontario through the Ontario Arts Council and the Ontario Media
Development Corporation for our publishing activities.

Cover art *Angélique* by Richard Horne, used by permission of the Black Studies Centre,
Montreal, Quebec.
Cover design: Jodi Armstrong

LIBRARY AND ARCHIVES CANADA CATALOGUING IN PUBLICATION

Gale, Lorena
Angélique

A play.
ISBN 978-0-88754-585-6
I. Title.

PS8563.A416A73 2000   C812'.54   C99-933117-5
PR9199.3.G254A73 2000

First edition: March 2000. Fifth printing: December 2010
Printed and bound in Canada by Gauvin Press, Gatineau

I dedicate this book to my mom, the late Lillian Madden,
who slaved all her life for minimum wage and still managed to house,
feed, clothe and educate 5 children. And to my son Clayton Cooper.
May he never know the hardships previous generations have endured.

ACKNOWLEDGEMENTS

The playwright acknowledges the assistance of: the 1997 Banff playRites Colony — a partnership between the Banff Centre, The Canada Council for the Arts, and Alberta Theatre Projects; The Canada Council for the Arts (Theatre Section); Canadian Heritage (Writing and Publishing); The Province of British Columbia (Recommender Program); as well as The Canadian Centre For Architecture, Women in View, National Arts Centre, Canadian Stage Company, Playwright's Theatre Centre, Nightwood Theatre Company, Western Canada Theatre Company, Headlines Theatre Company, Brenda Ledlay, Jackie Maxwell, Diane Roberts, Bob White, ahdri zhina mandela, Allison Sealy Smith, John Cooper, and Denyse Beaugrand Champagne.

Angélique was first produced by Alberta Theatre Projects, D. Michael Dobbin Producing Director, as part of the Pan Canadian play*Rites* '98 Festival, January 1998, with the following company:

THÉRÈSE	Tracey Ferencz
CLAUDE	Dennis Fitzgerald
FRANÇOIS	Andrew Gillies
IGNACE	Grant Linneberg
ANGÉLIQUE	Karen Robinson
MANON	Alexandra Thomson
CÉSAR	Nigel Shawn Williams

Directed by Sandhano Schultze
Set Design by Scott Reid
Costume Design by Judith Bowden
Lighting by Brian Pincourt
Stage Managed by Colin McCracken
Dramaturgy by Rob Moffatt

CHARACTERS

Marie Joseph Angélique: A slave, in a Canadian history book, (29).

François Poulin de Francheville: Montreal merchant, owner of the St. Maurice Ironworks and the slave Angélique, (40).

Thérèse de Couagne: Wife of François. A few years older than Angélique, (35)

Claude Thibault: The Francheville's indentured servant. Angélique's lover, (30's).

Ignace Gamelin: Entrepreneur/Montreal merchant. François' business partner, (40ish).

César: Slave owned by Ignace Gamelin. Lover to Angélique, (30's).

Manon: Indian slave owned by the de Berays, next door neighbours of the Franchevilles, (early 20's).

Reporter, **Margeurite**, **Hypolite**, **Marie Louise**, **Marie Josephe**, **Jean Josephe**, and **François de Beray**: These characters are to be played by the members of the main cast.

TIME

The present and 1730s. Then is now. Now is then.

PLACE

Montreal, 1700s.

NOTE

Unless otherwise stated, the slaves are working in every scene in which they appear, either in a modern or historical context. Although the specifics are not written into the text, what can be explored is the concept of witnessing. As servants and slaves are essentially invisible, experiment with who sees what, who knows what.

Angélique
by Lorena Gale

ACT I

Scene One

*The sound of African drumming. The featureless silhouette of
a woman dancing with a book against a backdrop of red, oranges
and yellow, suggestive of flames. VOICEOVER – building in
a rapid repetitive delivery.*

VOICEOVER
And in seventeen thirty-four a Negro slave set fire to the City of
Montreal and was hanged.
in seventeen thirty-four a Negro slave set fire to the City of Montreal
and was hanged.
seventeen thirty-four a Negro slave set fire to the City of Montreal
and was hanged.
a Negro slave set fire to the City of Montreal and was hanged
slave set fire to the City of Montreal and was hanged
set fire to the City of Montreal and was hanged
fire to the City of Montreal and was hanged
to the City of Montreal and was hanged
City of Montreal and was hanged
Montreal and was hanged
and was hanged
was hanged
hanged.

The crackling sound of fire.

Scene Two

*FRANÇOIS Poulin de Francheville in a pool of light. He is dressed
in full 18ᵗʰ century garb. He talks directly to the audience, with the
cocky confidence of a Donald Trump on a roll.*

FRANÇOIS
I was hot. I tell you, everything I touched would turn to gold. Or
should I say iron. The interest on the loans I paid out was rolling in.
And well... there seemed to be no end to the number of furs that

could be traded. Something went bing! in my mind. Iron… iron
is the wave of the future. So Ignace Gamelin and I laid down the
foundations for the Ironworks. Wrote to the Minister of Marine
requesting a twenty-year monopoly on the deposits in St. Maurice.
And ba-da-bing ba-da-bang! Request granted from the first day of
smelting! Not only that, but the right to exploit cultivated and
uncultivated lands next to my own. I felt like a king! Better than
Louis! I felt like Midas! With an iron touch. Which is better because
iron is stronger and sometimes more valuable than gold.

But do you think I can put a smile on my wife's face?

Our daughter, Marie Angélique, had been dead for two years. Still,
Thérèse cried all the time…. Don't get me wrong. I think of Marie
and I feel sad. Yes! But hey… life goes on. And we could always have
another child. *(beat)* Do you know how hard it is to get close to
someone who breaks into tears every time you touch her?

One day I met this really annoying little guy named Bleck. Nicholas
Bleck. A Flem. You know what they're like. Just arrived in New
France. "With a very rare and special cargo," he says. "Slaves. African
slaves. Not those wild things fresh from the jungle. But directly from
Portugal. Handsome servants experienced in the ways of Europeans
and trained to cater to our every pleasure." A luxury only a fine
gentleman like myself could appreciate. And a steal at any price.
I wasn't really interested. But the guy was so determined to make
a sale, I knew he wouldn't let me go before he displayed his
merchandise. So I said I'd take a look. What does it cost to look?

   ANGÉLIQUE in shadows.

The figure of this fine creature could not but attract my particular
notice. She was standing off to the side with some others. Perfectly
straight… with the most elegant shapes that can be viewed in nature.
Her chestnut skin shone with double luster. Her large ebony eyes
with their inward gaze. Her proud face… immobile… I don't
know…

Do you know what it's like to be flush? To say, "I want that!" And
without giving it any more thought, to just reach out and take it.
To be able to buy anything or anyone… there is no more powerful
feeling in the world! Eight hundred pounds later…

I thought maybe I could give this creature to Thérèse as a special surprise. Make her the envy of female society. Maybe she would be happy…. Want to be close…

What would you pay for your wife's happiness? What would you pay for your own?

Scene Three

Lighting change. ANGÉLIQUE, dressed in a white domestics uniform, in a spot. THÉRÈSE de Couagne dressed in early 18th century in another spot. ANGÉLIQUE directly addresses the audience as documentary, THÉRÈSE as commentary.

ANGÉLIQUE
Angélique… Marie Joseph…

THÉRÈSE
After my sister, Marie Joseph de Couagne.

ANGÉLIQUE
Angélique…

THÉRÈSE
After… *(Unable to speak the name of her dead daughter, she turns away.)*

ANGÉLIQUE
Negro slave born around 1710. Baptized in Montreal June 28, 1730. Hung in Montreal June 21, 1734.

THÉRÈSE
Property of François Poulin de Francheville. 427 rue St. Paul.

The lights come up. THÉRÈSE has been informing ANGÉLIQUE of her duties. She does so lightly and politely, but with the easy authority of one who is in command of her household. FRANÇOIS stands by her.

Beds each morning, change the linen every other day or so. Bathrooms every other morning. Vacuum the main living spaces— bedroom, living room, stairs—daily…. Don't worry. We have a deluxe machine. I hear it makes vacuuming a breeze…. Floors swept and washed every day. Waxing every third week. Are you getting all this?

ANGÉLIQUE
(eager to please) Oui, Madame.

THÉRÈSE
I am very sensitive to dust. You'll have to dust each day. Metal and wood surfaces polished. Mirrors and windows clear. Without streaks...

ANGÉLIQUE
Oui, Madame.

THÉRÈSE
Let's see. What else is there? Laundry, including dry cleaning, is Tuesday and Friday. Hand washing daily. Mending as necessary. Marketing is Saturday.

ANGÉLIQUE
Oui, Madame.

THÉRÈSE
We breakfast at eight, take luncheon at one and dine between six and six-thirty.

> CLAUDE, the Franchevilles' indentured servant, walks across the stage carrying a ladder. He wears modern clothing. THÉRÈSE notices him.

ANGÉLIQUE
Oui, Madame.

THÉRÈSE
Yours is the little room off the kitchen. Claude will show you where it is. Claude.... This is...

ANGÉLIQUE
Angélique...

THÉRÈSE
Yes.... See that she gets settled down to work.

CLAUDE
> *Oui*, Madame.

THÉRÈSE
> There is a place for everything in this house and everything has its place, do you understand?

ANGÉLIQUE
> Oh *oui*, Madame. I keep a very clean house. You will not be disappointed.

THÉRÈSE
> Good.

> *CLAUDE and ANGÉLIQUE exit.*

FRANÇOIS
> So…? What do you think?

THÉRÈSE
> Does it matter what I think?

FRANÇOIS
> Of course, Thérèse. Your opinions are important to me.

THÉRÈSE
> Then I think that we don't need a slave.

FRANÇOIS
> I didn't buy her because we needed her.

THÉRÈSE
> Why did you buy her?

FRANÇOIS
> Because…. Because I thought you would want one.

THÉRÈSE
> For me. *(beat)* Thank you. But next time, instead of asking what I think, try asking what I want. *(She exits.)*

FRANÇOIS
> *(to himself)* What do you want, Thérèse? What do you want?

Scene Four

*Jungle music on a boom box. "Agony" by Angie Angel. The
repetitive upbeat tempo like the accelerated drumming of a slave
driver. ANGÉLIQUE with a mop, moving though space in an
abstracted dervish of cleaning. CLAUDE and FRANÇOIS witness.*

ANGÉLIQUE
This time will be different.

This time everything will work out for me.
This time, I will not just
"live in."
This time, I will
"live with."
I'll make this strange new land – my land!
This house – my home!
These new people,
my people!
This time I will live in reasonable peace.

These people will be different.
These folk will be decent and good.
This mistress will be firm but gentle.
This master will be honest and fair.
There will be no
harsh looks or cruel words,
this time.
This time,
I will be treated with loving kindness and understanding.

I will work hard.
From sun to sun.
Do exactly as I'm told.
I will perform each duty with pride and obedience.
I will maintain their order.
Everything will go smoothly.
I'll know my place.

I will give freely of myself.
Repaying their humanity with loyalty.
Earning their protection and their care.
They'll wonder how they ever lived without me!

Life will be different this time.

There will be holidays…
and happy days…
and good times…
occasional laughter…
and private moments…
and…
and…

It will be good this time.

This time will be different.
This time will be different.
This time will be different.

Scene Five

*Light change. Night. FRANÇOIS sits at a small table with a candle
and a pitcher of water. CLAUDE and THÉRÈSE witness.*

FRANÇOIS
(whispers) Angélique… Angélique?

ANGÉLIQUE
Oui, Monsieur?

FRANÇOIS
Viens. Come.

ANGÉLIQUE
Is there something wrong, Monsieur?

FRANÇOIS
(trying to put her at ease) No, no. I just wanted… uh… pour me
a glass of water. Please.

ANGÉLIQUE
Oui, Monsieur.

*He watches intently as she goes to the table, pours him a glass,
which she sets beside him. He smiles at her and drinks. There is
a moment of awkward silence.*

Will that be all, Monsieur?

FRANÇOIS

Yes... uh... no. *(wanting her to like him)* I have something for you. A present. You like? *Castor.* Beaver. Its worth improves with wear. *Castor gras...* even more valuable. Not to mention warm. It's yours.

ANGÉLIQUE

(perplexed) Thank you, Monsieur.

FRANÇOIS

Don't mention it. *(putting the fur around her shoulders and considering her carefully a moment)* Now come.... Stand over here. I want to take a good look at you. *(There is yearning in his observation.)* Turn around. Slowly. That's it. Nice. Very nice. Yes.... You are a beauty... I wonder... *(with earnest curiosity)* Is it true what they say about African women?

ANGÉLIQUE

(stiffly) I'm sorry, Monsieur. I don't know what they say.

FRANÇOIS

That you're wilder? Freer? Hot like the sun that scorched you? *(She does not reply.)* I would like to know for myself...

ANGÉLIQUE

Please, Monsieur...

FRANÇOIS

No.... Don't fight it. You'll disturb Thérèse. *(She stops resisting.)* See? I'm not so bad. I'm better than sleeping in the snow. If you get my drift. *(beat)* Come on... smile. I will not hurt you. If you obey. I won't hurt you.

Scene Six

CLAUDE in a spot.

CLAUDE

This indenture made the 17th of August, 1729 between me, Claude Thibault, also known as Claude de la Butanne, aged 29 and François Poulin de Francheville witnesseth that I do covenant, promise and grant to François Poulin, from my first arrival at Montreal and after, for the term of three years, to serve in such service as he François Poulin shall there employ him.

> *ANGÉLIQUE enters and begins her cleaning dervish in silence. CLAUDE continues to speak as if he has been doing so for a while.*

Yep. This little piece of pounded wood is all that ties me here. One day I'm going to wipe my ass with this and stick it to Francheville's forehead. Take off across the river and not look back till the earth turns to sand beneath my feet and the sea stretches out unbroken before me!

ANGÉLIQUE
But why, Monsieur? What has Monsieur done to you?

CLAUDE
Nothing, I guess. I just don't plan on shovelling his horseshit for the rest of my life, that's all. Until then… I guess I'll just have another drink. *(takes a flask out of his shirt and drinks)* You want some? It's on the house.

ANGÉLIQUE
No thank you, Monsieur.

CLAUDE
Come on. Just take a swig. I hate to drink alone.

ANGÉLIQUE
But Madame…

CLAUDE
Fuck Madame! Yeesh! That's a scary thought. *(beat)* Just take a sip. It'll do you some good.

ANGÉLIQUE
If you insist, Monsieur.

CLAUDE
And drop the "Monsieur" bullshit. I'm not one of them. Call me Claude or call me Thibault as long as you call me, okay?

ANGÉLIQUE
You could be one of them. You look like one of them.

CLAUDE

Yeah, right. I guess to you we all look alike. No, don't confuse me with the rest of my species. I'm just a peon. Like you. Something to pee on. Cheers.

He drinks and hands the flask to her. She drinks.

ANGÉLIQUE

Look…! *(referring to an imaginary window)*

CLAUDE

The first snow is always the best. You see how it melts when it hits the ground. The earth isn't ready. Still too warm. It's not going to stick. Whatever falls will be gone by this afternoon. You see? It's already turning to rain. It will all get washed away. But the next time will be a blizzard and then you'll see.

ANGÉLIQUE

It's beautiful.

CLAUDE

You think so now, but after six or seven months of freezing your ass off you'll change your mind. Snow's a bitch. Let's drink to that.

ANGÉLIQUE

You drink too much.

CLAUDE

And you don't drink enough. *(He drinks.) Eau de Vie*! The spirit of life! Warms the soul, kills the pain! Here.

ANGÉLIQUE

I am not in pain.

CLAUDE

Keep telling yourself that and maybe one day you'll believe it. In the meantime, drink up.

ANGÉLIQUE

(drinks, then gives him back the flask) Claude? Where will you go? When your time is up?

CLAUDE

I don't know. Back to Franche Comte, maybe. Or the Islands. No snow in the Islands. Yeah…: The Islands… that's the place to be.

Warm winds, blue horizons, women running around naked all the time. That's what I hear. Is it true?

ANGÉLIQUE
How should I know?

CLAUDE
Sorry. I guess that's not the kind of question to ask a lady. But you can't blame a man for asking. *(beat)* I don't know. What island are you from?

ANGÉLIQUE
Not the ones you're thinking of. Madiere…. Across from Portugal. A jewel in the Atlantic.

CLAUDE
Sounds good to me. Maybe there. You want to come?

ANGÉLIQUE
Don't make me laugh.

CLAUDE
Why not? You're pretty when you laugh.

Scene Seven

Black. FRANÇOIS with a deer skin and a Bic lighter. He flicks. The light reveals him.

FRANÇOIS
(whispered) Angélique… Angélique?

Black. Beat. FRANÇOIS flicks again. The lights bump up. He is closer.

(whispered) Angélique… Angélique?

Black. FRANÇOIS with a deer skin.

(whispered) Angélique… Angélique?

ANGÉLIQUE in a spot.

ANGÉLIQUE
Angélique became the mistress of Jacques César, a Negro slave owned by Ignace Gamelin, with whom she had a son, Eustache, born in January 1730 and in May, 1732, she gave birth to twins; Louis and Marie Françoise.

Scene Eight

In the darkness we hear…

ANGÉLIQUE
(whispered) Brother? What are we doing here?

CÉSAR
Didn't they tell you?

ANGÉLIQUE
No.

> *Lights come up to reveal IGNACE Gamelin, in full period dress on one side of a two-way mirror. He speaks in a clinical, scientific manner.*

IGNACE
It's very interesting. Notice how they just stand there. It would seem like nothing is going on between them. But look… his eyes… her mouth. Fascinating. See. He is putting some distance between them in order to get a better look. *(beat)* I am surprised he's so contained. I've owned him for years and he hasn't had a woman.

FRANÇOIS
(enters the mirror) That you know of…

IGNACE
Touchée.

> *THÉRÈSE enters. The three are framed as if in portrait.*

THÉRÈSE
Why do they not speak, Ignace?

FRANÇOIS
Perhaps they are shy.

IGNACE

Perhaps they are like dogs. Two males pass on the street and they growl or bark to indicate status and territory. But a bitch in heat struts past and the first thing that happens is they sniff each other out. Circle and sniff. Most animals do that. Hey François, maybe we should make a study of this. The unusual mating practices of the African in captivity. Imagine, we could be scholars as well as merchants.

FRANÇOIS

(guarded jealousy) She won't go for him…

THÉRÈSE

Why not? I would… *(The men turn to her.)* If I were her.

IGNACE

Care to place a little wager? *(takes out his purse)*

FRANÇOIS

I hate to take your money.

THÉRÈSE

Shh…

IGNACE

The sniffing has begun.

> *The lights come up on ANGÉLIQUE and CÉSAR, IGNACE's slave.*
> *They whisper.*

CÉSAR

My master says that you are to be with me now.

ANGÉLIQUE

What!

THÉRÈSE

What are they saying?

IGNACE

Look.

CÉSAR

You have been chosen for me.

ANGÉLIQUE

I don't even know you.... And we're supposed to!?

CÉSAR

I guess.

ANGÉLIQUE

What if I refuse?

CÉSAR

I don't know.

ANGÉLIQUE

And you agreed to this?

CÉSAR

It's been a long time, Sister. I don't come into contact with too many of our people. Let alone women. *(pause)* I need... someone.

ANGÉLIQUE

And any one will do?

CÉSAR

Someone...

ANGÉLIQUE

Then you are no better than they are! *(beat)* Come on. Let's get this over with. *(lying down, opening her legs)* This is what it's all about? Well, take it. Here it is. Come on and take it. Just take it. I won't fight you. I've been chosen for you. Well, here I am. Only make it fast. I don't have all day. I have other work I have to do.

IGNACE

Alright César, old boy! The sexual prowess of the African male is legendary. Let this be a lesson to you François. Don't bet with the best 'cause the best only bet on a sure thing. Those two will turn a profit for us in no time. *(FRANÇOIS reaches for his purse.)* Oh.... Put that away. We are, after all, gentlemen.

> *The two men exit. Lights out on THÉRÈSE who watches with fascination.*

ANGÉLIQUE

Well? What are you waiting for?

CÉSAR

Get up off of that floor. You think I want it to be like this?

ANGÉLIQUE

I don't care what you think.

CÉSAR

What am I supposed to do? Just say no? All I did was ask permission to court a woman. I thought he'd just let me find one on my own. There's an Indian girl I see sometimes. I guess my master thought he was doing me a favour.

ANGÉLIQUE

Real generous of him.

CÉSAR

Real generous of your master, for he would have to give permission too. If it makes you feel any better, now that I've seen you up close I'm not much taken by you either. But we've been paired together. And there is no getting away from it.

ANGÉLIQUE

(pause) What do we do?

CÉSAR

Make the best of it, I guess. We can start by trying to be friends. Yes? Maybe we can pretend that we are meeting again. In another time, another place. Under more pleasant circumstances. Yes? Sister? *(He pretends.)* Hello. Wonderful woman of the great homeland. I haven't seen you before. I am César. Jacques César.

ANGÉLIQUE

I am… Angélique. Marie Joseph Angélique.

Scene Nine

The painful sounds of childbirth. IGNACE and FRANÇOIS are smoking and waiting. CLAUDE in the shadows. CÉSAR waits expectantly off in a corner. CÉSAR jumps up.

IGNACE

Relax, old man. There is nothing you can do. You will only be in the way. The women have everything under control…

THÉRÈSE
(*off*) It's a boy...!

FRANÇOIS
A boy...

IGNACE
It's a boy! Congratulations, César old man. Or should I say Papa.

CÉSAR
Merci, Monsieur. I am very proud to have a son.

IGNACE
If he is anything like you César, he'll be a strong lad.

FRANÇOIS
And a strong man. He'll fetch a good price when the time comes.

IGNACE
You scoundrel. Don't run off with the profits. I lay claim to half.

THÉRÈSE
(*enters with a bundle*) It's a boy, François.

FRANÇOIS
Beautiful.

> *He turns away. She addresses CÉSAR.*

THÉRÈSE
Would you like to hold him?

CÉSAR
Thank you, Madame.

> *She delicately hands the baby to CÉSAR. They admire it in silence for a moment.*

IGNACE
(*looking at the baby*) He's awfully fair. (*They all turn to him.*) Which only goes to show that everything is born pure. Perfect! (*beat*) His face all screwed up like that – you know who he reminds me of?

FRANÇOIS
(quickly) Who?

IGNACE
Eustache, the foreman at the Ironworks.

FRANÇOIS
Eustache?

IGNACE
All this baby is missing is his moustache.

FRANÇOIS
(relieved) Yes… *(laughs)* Yes, it does look like Eustache. All red face and hairy. Then that's what we will call it. Eustache.

IGNACE
(to CÉSAR) Well, we better be heading back. Plenty of time to play daddy ahead of you.

FRANÇOIS
Claude. See to Monsieur Gamelin's carriage.

CLAUDE
Oui, Monsieur. *(exits)*

IGNACE
By the way, how is the mother doing?

THÉRÈSE
Fine. She's just fine.

IGNACE
Now hand him back.

> *CÉSAR hands the baby to THÉRÈSE.*

FRANÇOIS
I'll see you to the door.

> *They exit. THÉRÈSE is left holding the baby. She studies its face.*

Scene Ten

ANGÉLIQUE alone with her baby. The sound of a new heart beating. She stands, gently swaying, rocking the child in her arms.

ANGÉLIQUE
In the beginning there was Darkness.
Dense
profound
Darkness.
Like a thick black blanket
stretching
into seamless infinity.
Darkness was all and all was Darkness.
Is.
And would ever be.
And Darkness slumbered,
complete
in her ebony world.

'Til one day there was a movement, a stirring, a rumbling
somewhere
deep inside.
An unacknowledged longing to be
more
than everything.
Growing like the sound of distant thunder.
Unsettling her dreams,
but not enough to wake her.

The stirring grew into a churning.
The darkness swirled and eddied.
Rising
and crashing
in
on herself.
She rocked.
She reeled.
Until she woke .
And then she knew
that she would
never
sleep again.

"Something has changed in me. I can no longer bear to be alone."

And with that thought,
Darkness heaved and pushed.
Heaved and pushed.
Forcing
desire from her depths.
Giving birth to
Light.

Light was small.
No bigger than a spark.
But in It,
Darkness could
see
the full extent of herself.

"I am so much more than what I thought I was."

And Light blinked
with the bright eyes of a new born.
Dazzling.
Delighting Darkness.
And a great heat she had never before noticed
spread through Darkness
as she closed
protectively
around Light. Like
mother
cradling
child.

Light,
unlike Darkness,
came into being
complete
with its own self knowledge
which it fed on with a ferocious hunger,
growing fatter,
and pushing back
Darkness in defiance.

Darkness,
being everywhere, still

encompassed Light no matter how she strained
to give It room.

Light,
fueled by it's own existence, grew
hotter
in confinement.

"I am so much more than what I am. At least as much as Darkness,
which is everywhere. Why must I be contained? Without me
Darkness has no Knowledge of itself. Therefore, I am everything!
And Darkness is nothing!

Light burned with greater arrogance.
Growing hotter and denser with a simmering anger,
which bubbled
and popped
beneath its surface of brilliance.
And still
Darkness
closed around it.

"I am more... I am more than... I am more than this," Light
seethed.

'Til it was so
full
of itself
It exploded.
Sending shards of its being
hurling through Darkness.
Lighting up
the void.

Light
was now everywhere.
Cutting through darkness with the sharpness of
an axe.
Cruelly
severing
the umbilicus between them.

Darkness
was so blinded by the light

she could no longer
see,
and so retreated
to where she could have some sense of herself.
Though light still pierced her,
as a reminder that It
now
ruled
every
thing.

Light and Darkness.

That is how the two became separate forces.
In constant opposition.
Light in the forefront
and Darkness...
waiting...
on the edge
of everything.

But there is something else we know, my child. That in the end, Darkness reclaims everything. The stars will fall. The sun will cease to shine. Light will collapse in on itself. 'Til once again, it is nothing more than just a little spark. That flickers. Sputters. Pops itself out. Then Darkness will resume her peaceful reign.

That day is a long way off. I will ever see it. Neither will you, my baby.... So light.... So powerfully dark.

VOICEOVER
(whispered) Angélique... Angélique?

> *Puts her hand over the baby's face, smothering it. The heartbeat stops. Silence.*

Fly home and greet the darkness. There are others waiting there. Mama loves you and will join you soon.

> *THÉRÈSE enters. She regards ANGÉLIQUE compassionately and speaks from her own pain.*

THÉRÈSE
Children don't live too long here. Most babies born in the winter don't live to see the spring. I don't know why.... Best it happened

early on. That way you don't get too attached. *(looks at the dead baby)* I had a child once.... A girl. Marie Angélique. Eight winters she lasted. Eight sweet years.... And then she caught a fever she was just too young to fight.... So you're lucky it happened sooner.

Scene Eleven

FRANÇOIS looking over a file folder of documents. THÉRÈSE regards him for a tense moment, then begins tentatively.

THÉRÈSE
God forgive me, but I am glad it's dead. *(no response)* At least now we don't have to bear the embarrassment of her bastard running around the streets. *(He pays little attention.)* I find it difficult to believe that César was the father... the baby was so pale.

FRANÇOIS
(still engrossed in his work) What does it matter? It's dead now. It's gone.

THÉRÈSE
Do you know who the father was?

FRANÇOIS
César.

THÉRÈSE
No.

FRANÇOIS
Then how should I know? It could be anyone for all we know. Claude even...

THÉRÈSE
Or you...

Pause.

FRANÇOIS
(laughs) Really, Thérèse. I have more important things to worry about.

THÉRÈSE
(softly) I have wrestled with that possibility since that child was born. *(beat)* I understand how tempting it could be… when it is so readily available. To succumb to temptation…

FRANÇOIS
I don't think I like what you are implying.

THÉRÈSE
(quickly) Did you?

FRANÇOIS
Did I what?

THÉRÈSE
(pause) I think we should get rid of her, François.

FRANÇOIS
And what do you propose I should do with her?

THÉRÈSE
Sell her. Give her away.

FRANÇOIS
Just give her away?

THÉRÈSE
I don't know. Anything. Just get her out of here.

FRANÇOIS
Why?

THÉRÈSE
Because I'm your wife and I am asking you.

FRANÇOIS
(irritated) You're being ridiculous. What's gotten into you, Thérèse? First you accuse me of being an adulterer and now you want me to give up a valuable piece of property just because of some crazy idea you've got?

THÉRÈSE
Please, François.

FRANÇOIS

(after a beat, softer) Listen to me. You are my wife. I love you. Believe me when I tell you that you have nothing to worry about. *(kisses her forehead)* Now, all this nonsense has interrupted my work. I'm going off to collect my thoughts.

THÉRÈSE

François…. Tell me you will consider it? Out of respect for me?

FRANÇOIS

You have nothing to worry about.

Scene Twelve

The sound of one lone drum beating in a slow native rhythm. MANON, a panisse, a young native slave/servant carries a basket of wet clothes. ANGÉLIQUE enters with a basket of wet clothes, notices MANON and halts. She stares. ANGÉLIQUE returns her gaze with similar curiosity. Another drum beating to a corresponding African rhythm joins with the first. They do not clash. They complement. MANON puts her basket down and starts to shake and hang the clothing at the opposite end of the clothesline to ANGÉLIQUE. As she does so she begins to sing to herself in her native language. It is a mournful song. ANGÉLIQUE starts to hang her wash and once again responds to MANON singing with her own song in an African language. The two songs blend in a call and response style and in rhythm to the beating of the two drums. The women work and sing. All the while getting closer and closer. Freer and freer. Becoming jubilant. They meet in the centre, neither capable of hanging more clothes. They regard each other for a moment. They smile in their song, uncomfortable but friendly. They are about to speak when THÉRÈSE enters.

THÉRÈSE

Stop. Stop that noise immediately. *(tearing the laundry from the line in her anger)* How many times do I have to tell you that it's strictly forbidden. I should have you both whipped. Maybe then you would understand that we are a civilized people and won't tolerate that sort of… savage behaviour. *(to MANON)* Now you get out of here. And don't think I won't mention this to Madame de Beray, because I will.

Scene Thirteen

*ANGÉLIQUE drags a carpet or a panel of heavy drapes or a
manageable wall tapestry out and hangs it over the line.
THÉRÈSE waits silently while ANGÉLIQUE toils. When
ANGÉLIQUE is finished, she stands beside the hanging. THÉRÈSE
then commences to beat the rug, each blow being a complete and
separate beating in itself, meted out over the course of time.
ANGÉLIQUE responds as if she herself is being struck – first with
pain, then with growing endurance and compressed rage.
FRANÇOIS enters and watches from the side and MANON
watches from the shadows.*

THÉRÈSE
Because you dropped the serving bowl. *(smack)*
Because you were late coming back from the market. *(smack)*
Because you forgot to put oil in the lamps. *(smack)*
Because you were whistling in the kitchen. *(smack)*

ANGÉLIQUE
Each stroke a reminder.

THÉRÈSE
Because the bread didn't rise. *(smack)*
Because he went to you again last night. *(smack)*
Because you burnt the edges of the waffles. *(smack)*
Because he is my husband and I love him. *(smack)*

ANGÉLIQUE
Each stroke a reminder.

THÉRÈSE
Because he stared at you through dinner. *(smack)*
Because I have to pretend this isn't happening. *(smack)*
Because I wish you'd disappear. *(smack)*
Because there is nothing else I can do. *(smack)*

THÉRÈSE crosses to FRANÇOIS and they exit together.

ANGÉLIQUE
Each stroke…

Scene Fourteen

ANGÉLIQUE is drinking Eau de Vie. *CÉSAR is rubbing her back.*

CÉSAR
...eleven times, this slave and his Indian wife. Ten times they ran away. Ten times they were caught. First time they got caught, the master cut off one of their feet. Next time a hand. Next time an ear. Next time a nose. Next time... whatever. These two so cut up makes you wonder how they were still standing. But the eleventh time... *(He finishes rubbing her down.)* Hey... slow down. *(He takes the flask from her.)* There. *(He pats her stomach.)* This one is mine and I don't want nothing to happen to it.

ANGÉLIQUE
Well, you just march up there and tell that to Madame. Say, "Madame, I want you to give my Angélique the day off." She'll laugh in your face. These people work me harder than they work their horses. *(cautiously)* Do you remember what it was like before?

CÉSAR
Before what?

ANGÉLIQUE
Before...

CÉSAR
I have no before. I don't remember my mama or my papa. Probably sold or died off before I could get a good fix on 'em. I got sold to a fur trader when I was still a boy, and come up north. Been here ever since.

ANGÉLIQUE
I remember. Before this Montreal. This New France. Before this Canada. I remember Madiere. Picking coffee with my mother and my father. The coffee beans. Their tender green. Their firmness between my little fingers. We toiled for them. Yes! But it was work. Just work. Hard work is a part of life. And at least we were together.

On the days of rest and celebration we would all descend on the beach. We would build a fire in conjunction to the line of the horizon. As the sun set, the orange and red and yellow of day's transition into night, would blend with the colours in the fire. Everyone would gather round. And to the beating of a drum, they would tell the stories of our ancestors. Our warriors dancing the great battles. Our hunters re-enacting their kills.

The little me would stand on the sandy shore and look out across the inky water. And imagine I could see the land of my ancestors. It was that close. It was that far away. *(pause)* I cannot understand this coldness and this cruelty. I may have always been a slave. But I did not feel like one until I came to this land… *(carefully)* We could run.

CÉSAR

(laughs) Sure. You wait here while I pack my belongings. Hey! I've got everything. Let's go!

ANGÉLIQUE

We could!

CÉSAR

Look Angélique, everywhere we go we're going to be slaves. There's nowhere to hide. And even if there was we can't hide forever. They'll find us. Snap the chains back on or worse. I don't fancy clomping around the rest of my life with one foot. Gamelin isn't too bad a master. And I have you now. And a baby coming. It may not seem like too much. But the one thing I have learned, is to take what happiness I can when I can get it. And everything I have is right here.

ANGÉLIQUE

But don't you want to be your own man? Wake up in the morning and decide what you want to do…

CÉSAR

I am just trying to accept what life has put before me.

ANGÉLIQUE

Accept…

CÉSAR

That's right. Accept. 'Cause there is nothing I can say or do that's going to change my lot in this life. If I am going to have any kind of happiness I have to come to terms with that fact. I suggest you do too. Find some way to live. Something to live for. And life will seem a little easier.

ANGÉLIQUE

But what about those eleven times? Don't they tell you something.

CÉSAR
Yeah. They made it the eleventh time. Into heaven. They were found wrapped in each other's arms. Froze to death. In the snow.

FRANÇOIS
(whispers off) Angélique? Angélique?

CÉSAR
Just take what happiness you can – when you can.

Scene Fifteen

Light change.

CÉSAR
Eustache. Natural son of Marie Joseph Angélique and Jacques César. Baptised, January 11, 1731. Buried, Feb. 12. 1731. Age…

ANGÉLIQUE
One month.

CÉSAR
Louis: *fils naturel de la meme negresse* and brother of the previous. Born and baptized May 26, 1732. Buried the next day. Age…

ANGÉLIQUE
Two days.

CÉSAR
Marie Françoise, twin sister of the preceding. Buried October 29, 1732. Age…

ANGÉLIQUE
Five months.

CÉSAR
Father – unknown. Though the mother declared it to be Jacques César. *(CÉSAR exits.)*

Scene Sixteen

FRANÇOIS enters and stands behind ANGÉLIQUE. CLAUDE works quietly in the background. Every once in a while he looks in the direction of ANGÉLIQUE. He is aware of what is happening with her but cannot watch openly. From behind, FRANÇOIS reaches around and removes ANGÉLIQUE's uniform, revealing period undergarments beneath her modern clothing. He then commences to dress her up again, only this time, in period clothing. ANGÉLIQUE does not resist.

ANGÉLIQUE
A dog barking…. A baby crying…. Footsteps…
The wind whistling low and breathy…

> *THÉRÈSE enters and watches in the shadows.*

The faint creek of wood giving way to weight…
Someone stepping stealthily on the fourth floorboard
before the doorway to my room.
There is no sneaking in this house where every sound
betrays.
A cat scowling…
Perhaps the dog has caught the cat.
Or maybe,
the cat has caught the dog.

> *FRANÇOIS places a corset on ANGÉLIQUE.*

I could leave here. Right now!

> *She takes a step away from him. Then another and another which has the effect of tightening the corset.*

I am walking towards the door… I am opening it… I am stepping
outside and…

> *She falls forward. Her arms spread like a bird. She is kept aloft by the laces of the corset which FRANÇOIS holds like reins on a wild horse. But he doesn't notice anything that's happening with her. He pumps her, like he's fucking her from behind.*

I'm freeeeeeee! I'm free! I'm free! I'm free! Look at meeee! I'm
running through the gates of the city. I'm racing across the land.

I'm floating across the big river. I am washed up on the shores of my beloved Madiere...

He pulls her back to him and ties the corset.

But I am not really out there...

She steps into the dress.

I am here.
I see.

The dog has caught the cat. The cat has a mouse in its jaws. The mouse is playing dead.

You think you own me. This body. That complies. That never fights. The heat you feel is white-hot rage scorching the inside of my mind. A blazing fury I bite back. Fire – I would spit into your face. If you would face me you coward, you would know.... One day...

Scene Seventeen

CLAUDE whistles cheerfully to himself, carries two pails of water which we are to believe he has hauled from a well. He carries them to a large black kettle and pours them in. He speaks with great caution, as he works.

CLAUDE
There's a place. Not too far from here. South. Called New England. Ever heard of it? *(She does not respond.)* I went there once with Monsieur Francheville. Not much different from here. Only everyone speaks English. And free Blacks too.

ANGÉLIQUE
(cautiously) How do you know they're free?

She takes up her old clothing and puts it in the kettle.

CLAUDE
We took the horses to the blacksmith. Right next door was a small house. In need of some repair. But it looked safe. Three little African children playing in the yard. I figured they must be his.

ANGÉLIQUE

That doesn't make them free. Makes them children.

Takes a bucket and pours it in the kettle.

CLAUDE

He spoke to Monsieur Francheville directly. Monsieur paid him directly, though he complained about the price. Every man who came into the smithy's shouted at him like he was their slave. But when they left they paid him like a free man.

ANGÉLIQUE

How do you know his master didn't hire him out? Make himself more money?

CLAUDE

I don't. But I'm willing to wager that I'm right and you're wrong.

ANGÉLIQUE

I'm not willing to bet my body parts on your view of the world.

CLAUDE

(serious) I'll prove it. It's about two, maybe three weeks journey. Depending on time of year, weather. Weather's great now. Let's go. I know the way.

ANGÉLIQUE

We can't just walk out of here.

CLAUDE

It's that easy. Just put one foot in front of the other. Come on. I'll show you.

ANGÉLIQUE

Why? Why should I trust you?

He takes her hand and kisses it.

FRANÇOIS

(off) Angélique! Angélique…

CLAUDE

Any time you want out… I know the way.

FRANÇOIS enters.

FRANÇOIS
Angélique… *(surprised)* Oh, Claude…

ANGÉLIQUE takes a bucket and pours it in the kettle.

CLAUDE
What can I do for you, Monsieur?

FRANÇOIS
Uh…. The Mercedes. I think you should take it in and have it looked at.

CLAUDE
Sure thing.

He lights a fire under the kettle.

You leaving town again?

FRANÇOIS
Soon. Real soon.

He regards CLAUDE with cloaked suspicion. ANGÉLIQUE takes a bucket and pours it into the kettle.

Angélique…. Watching you pour that water has made me real thirsty. Why don't you go and get me a cup.

ANGÉLIQUE
Oui, Monsieur. *(She exits.)*

FRANÇOIS
You're a really useful guy to have around the house.

CLAUDE
That's why you pay me the big bucks.

FRANÇOIS
Yeah, well, maybe you should come out with me to the Ironworks. We could use someone like you out there.

CLAUDE
What about Madame? How will she cope?

FRANÇOIS
Is it Madame you're concerned for? Or Angélique?

> *ANGÉLIQUE enters. CLAUDE notices but doesn't say anything.*

You've been fucking her, haven't you?

CLAUDE
No, Monsieur.

FRANÇOIS
But you want to.

> *She spits in the water. Stirs it with her finger.*

I don't blame you. Everyone should get a taste of brown sugar.

ANGÉLIQUE
Your water, Sir.

FRANÇOIS
(with great show) Why, thank you. *(to CLAUDE)* Salute. *(He drinks.)* Mmmm. That was the coolest, sweetest water I ever tasted. Thanks again. *(smiles at ANGÉLIQUE and tosses CLAUDE the keys)* I want the car back in two hours. Get moving.

CLAUDE
Excuse me, Sir...

FRANÇOIS
What!

CLAUDE
It might save you some money if you showed me exactly what the problem is. You know. Mechanics.

FRANÇOIS
Don't worry about the money.

CLAUDE
But it might be something I can fix myself.

FRANÇOIS
Jesus, Claude…

CLAUDE
Unless, of course, Monsieur is engaged in more pressing business…

FRANÇOIS regards CLAUDE for a moment. Then ANGÉLIQUE.

FRANÇOIS
Yeah…. Right. *(finishes his water)* Let's go.

They exit. ANGÉLIQUE picks up a long stick and stirs the laundry.

ANGÉLIQUE
Mistah buckra
he get sick
he tak fever
he be die.
he be die

Scene Eighteen

IGNACE Gamelin in a pool of light. Delivers the following as in eulogy.

IGNACE
François Poulin de Francheville. Merchant, fur trader, seigneur and entrepreneur in the Saint Maurice Ironworks. Son of Michel Poulin and Marie Jutras. Brother to Pierre Poulin and loving husband to Thérèse de Couagne. And, of course, my dearest friend and business partner. Born October 7, 1692. Died November 3, 1733. His early death is a grave loss to this colony.

Light expands to reveal THÉRÈSE in a black business suit and a stylish black hat with the netting pulled over her face.

THÉRÈSE
I loved him, Ignace.

IGNACE
I know, my dear.

THÉRÈSE

From the first moment I saw him. I was taking a bucket of ashes around back to the stables. We'd had a visit by *les Lutins* the night before. And I had heard that the only way to get rid of these mischievous goblins was to put a pail of ashes just inside the stable door. Because *les Lutins* hate ashes. And that would discourage them from ever coming again.

I heard someone coming to the stables. I wasn't expecting visitors. I thought the goblins were back. I didn't want them to catch me. So I hid. *(She laughs at the memory.)* Well, François opened the stable door – ashes went flying everywhere! And François cursed. *Mon Dieu,* I had never heard anything like it before. And then he started to stamp. I didn't realize it but some of the ashes were live and catching in the hay that lined the stable floor. All I could hear was this stamping and cursing and I thought for sure it was the goblins. So I grabbed a pitch fork and went charging out from my cache. Only to find a very strong and handsome young man stamping out the sparks. We were married six months later.

IGNACE

He loved you. He was my best friend and I know. In spite of everything he always loved you dearly.

THÉRÈSE

In spite of everything.

IGNACE

Believe it. He leaves his heart behind with you.

THÉRÈSE

What will I do, Ignace? How will I get by?

IGNACE

He left you well provided for. In addition to this property there is the farm in the parish of Saint Michel. And as his wife you inherit his interests in the St. Maurice Ironworks, which include his own investments, the seigneury of Saint Maurice, and a small annual income derived from his having contributed to the lands as a capitol asset. Although there isn't much cash, you should never have to worry. You would receive a generous sum should you choose to liquidate any or all of these assets.

THÉRÈSE

I know. I know.

IGNACE
There is someone who would be interested in taking the Ironworks off your hands. His name is Cugnet and he…

THÉRÈSE
I don't want to sell the Ironworks, Ignace.

IGNACE
But it is a tricky business. And the complexities are better managed by those who are knowledgeable in the field.

THÉRÈSE
Then I will learn.

IGNACE
But it would only drain your energy at a time when you should be mourning your husband.

THÉRÈSE
I feel I must carry out his work. I know how important the Ironworks were to François. Perhaps by retaining them, I keep a part of him I never had. By working with you I will get to learn a part of him I never knew. You will advise me, won't you Ignace?

IGNACE
Well, yes, but… Thérèse… I know you're not thinking clearly with François' death so fresh in your heart. Rest. Think it over. I'll call again in a few days or so. I'm sure that in time you will see that unburdening yourself of the Ironworks is the most reasonable decision… *(calls)* Angélique.

ANGÉLIQUE
Oui, Monsieur Gamelin.

IGNACE
Take care of La Dame de Francheville.

He kisses THÉRÈSE on the forehead.

Remember, my dear. He always loved you.

IGNACE exits. The two women are alone. There is a long awkward silence. ANGÉLIQUE, her eyes downcast, stands waiting for some order, as THÉRÈSE regards her with a mixed range of emotions.

THÉRÈSE
(with a genuine desire to know) Tell me something?

ANGÉLIQUE
Oui, Madame.

THÉRÈSE
(with difficulty but without malice) Did you like it? *(beat)* When he came to you at night?

ANGÉLIQUE
No, Madame.

THÉRÈSE
All this time?

ANGÉLIQUE
No, Madame.

THÉRÈSE
Why didn't you come to me?

ANGÉLIQUE
You have punished me for less, Madame.

THÉRÈSE
I have punished you because…. You could have stopped him. You could have tried to stop him.

ANGÉLIQUE
So could you. He was your husband. The master only took from me what you refused to give.

THÉRÈSE
(She advances on ANGÉLIQUE and in her anger, begins to slap her around.) You ungrateful, jealous, slut. Black bitch. Lying whore. You liked it when he took you. You nigger girls are good for nothing else. You liked it. So don't you lie to me. You liked it.

ANGÉLIQUE
(grabs her hands) And you didn't. You sent him to me. The fault is yours Madame. Not mine. *(letting her go)* I know that you have lost yourself in grief. I know the anger and the rage of loss. How hard it is to contain. How it needs to unleash itself on something. But I'm

not going to let you beat it out on me. Do you understand? Do not strike me again.

THÉRÈSE
(*collapses in her grief and tears*) François... François...

ANGÉLIQUE
He's gone, Madame. It's just you now. So you have to be strong.
(*ANGÉLIQUE cradles her.*) That's right. Let it out. Let it all out.
I know that things haven't been good between us. But that's all going to change now. I'll serve you well. If you will let me. I will serve you.

ACT II

Scene One

MANON in a spot.

MANON

La negresse semble de laisser ce premier amant, César, pour tomber dans les bras d'un blanc, Claude Thibault.

CLAUDE outside in a gentle snow. He speaks as if ANGÉLIQUE is there.

CLAUDE

The thing about snow is that even though together on the ground it all looks the same – each snowflake is different. Each has its own size, shape. Its own tiny crystal pattern. *(trying to catch one)* There. See? Aw, it melted. *(tries again)* Heat is its mortal enemy. So you have to be quick. 'Cause alone, the lifetime of a snowflake is brief. But together, one can last a whole winter. That's why, two, or three, or four or more catch on to each other and fall together. Even snow wants to live… as best as it can.

ANGÉLIQUE enters with her hands behind her back.

ANGÉLIQUE

I like how it makes everything quiet. But what I like most about snow is… snowballs!

She throws one at him.

CLAUDE

Why you…!

He chases her around playfully. She squeals. He catches her. They fall to the ground, laughing. He kisses her briefly. She kisses him passionately. MANON creeps in and watches them from the shadows.

We should be getting back.

ANGÉLIQUE

You go. I want to stay a little while longer.

CLAUDE
I'm not going anywhere without you.

> *CLAUDE sings a vibrant and raucous French folk song, such as "En Roulant Ma Boule Roulant." He claps and stamps his feet. ANGÉLIQUE laughs. He grabs her and tries to dance with her.*

ANGÉLIQUE
Stop! Stop! Stop! Stop!

CLAUDE
You don't like to dance.

ANGÉLIQUE
I can't dance like that. All left feet and straight lines.

CLAUDE
If you just tried a little you would get the hang of it.

ANGÉLIQUE
I have tried. My body refuses to move in that way.

CLAUDE
But I can't dance alone.

ANGÉLIQUE
Why not?

CLAUDE
I don't know. It just doesn't seem right – if there is someone to dance with.

> *He tries to dance with her again.*

ANGÉLIQUE
No.

CLAUDE
Won't you at least try?

ANGÉLIQUE
No.

CLAUDE
Then you show me.

ANGÉLIQUE
What?

CLAUDE
Show me a dance, that you would dance, if you wanted to dance with someone.

ANGÉLIQUE
You would only find it strange.

CLAUDE
No stranger than you find my dancing. Teach me your steps so that I can dance with you.

ANGÉLIQUE
Well, for that we would need a drum, which is forbidden. How can I dance without a drum?

CLAUDE
I can beat out a rhythm for you.

> *He starts to beat on the ground.*

ANGÉLIQUE
No, no, no… not like that. Like this.

> *She beats out a simple rhythm on her clothing. He tries. She shakes her head.*

Imagine that you are a drum. Deep and resonant. And the rhythm is the beating of your heart when your spirit is in flight.

> *She continues beating on herself. He tries again.*

Yes! You catch on quick.

CLAUDE
No flies on me.

> *ANGÉLIQUE laughs and beats a new rhythm which he follows.*

ANGÉLIQUE
First you take off like a startled bird. Fluttering with surprise. But as your wings take you higher into the safety of the sky, they calm... and beat with a certain, steady pace.

As she speaks, she gradually stops beating on herself as her rhythms are taken up by the real drum.

Yes.... Up. Up you fly. Your heart thumps loud. Deliberate. Pumping rhythm through your veins. You soar up to the sun. You spiral down to the ground. You careen on the slightest of air. You move... unfettered... through time and space. There is just the beating of your heart and the beating of the drum taking your body anywhere it wants to go.

She dances, the drums beat, the snow falls around her, and CLAUDE watches with obvious sensual delight. He goes to her and tries move with her, but he can't keep up. CÉSAR enters and watches. CLAUDE grabs ANGÉLIQUE and kisses her.

ANGÉLIQUE
Look. It stopped snowing.

CÉSAR
Angélique.

ANGÉLIQUE
(stepping back from CLAUDE) César.

CÉSAR
I went looking for you at the house. But your mistress didn't know where you were.

ANGÉLIQUE
I better go see if she needs anything.

CLAUDE
I'll go.

CÉSAR
You wait a minute.

CLAUDE pauses.

ANGÉLIQUE
César...

CÉSAR
I want you to stay away from her. You understand.

ANGÉLIQUE
César...

CÉSAR
I catch you sniffing around her again...

CLAUDE
You'll what? Eh? What are you going to do? *(after CÉSAR says nothing)* Yeah, that's what I thought.

ANGÉLIQUE
Claude.... Please?

CLAUDE
Sure.

> *He kisses her while looking at CÉSAR.*

You need anything, just shout. *(exits)*

CÉSAR
He the reason I don't see you any more?

ANGÉLIQUE
César...

CÉSAR
You haven't had enough of one white man you have to have another? *(as he takes out a flask of* Eau de Vie*)* And where are you getting this from? Is he giving it to you? No wonder you're acting like you do.

ANGÉLIQUE
And how am I acting?

CÉSAR
Like a drunken whore.

ANGÉLIQUE

Thank you, Brother.

CÉSAR

Look. It's just…. We're supposed to be together. We have to stick together.

ANGÉLIQUE

Only reason we're together is our masters say so. My master is dead. And I don't plan on replacing him any time soon.

CÉSAR

Your Mistress isn't.

ANGÉLIQUE

She doesn't pay no mind to what I do.

CÉSAR

What about me? What am I supposed to do?

ANGÉLIQUE

I don't care what you do, César.

CÉSAR

We're in this together. You can't choose that white man over me?

ANGÉLIQUE

I don't choose you at all! No more than you chose me! If there were five more to choose from you still wouldn't choose me. I'm just all there is. Better than nothing. Claude has a choice. He chooses me.

CÉSAR

Oh, I see. You think you're special. He loves you…. Dream on. Haven't you been a slave long enough to know that there is only one thing a white man wants from a slave woman.

ANGÉLIQUE

Claude isn't like that. He's different.

CÉSAR

Yeah. Like he's refusing what you're giving out.

ANGÉLIQUE

Yes. I don't give anything. He doesn't take.

CÉSAR

Doesn't mean he don't want.

ANGÉLIQUE

Doesn't mean I won't give. *(beat)* I have been a slave long enough to realize you have to take what happiness you can when you can. Isn't that what you said César?

CÉSAR

Yeah. That's what I said. You're making a big mistake. There's only one thing worse than a rich white master and that's poor white who wants to be one. You think he's on your side right now. But watch out. 'Cause in the end they are all white together.

CÉSAR exits. MANON follows him. He pushes her away.

Scene Two

ANGÉLIQUE in light. CLAUDE in shadow.

CLAUDE

Deep.

ANGÉLIQUE

I want to be close. To feel love. Choose love. Give…

CLAUDE

Rich.

ANGÉLIQUE

Dare I? Trust? Hope?

CLAUDE

Dark.

ANGÉLIQUE

Dare I? Give?

CLAUDE

Ripe.

ANGÉLIQUE

Yes!

CLAUDE
(coming into the light) Mine!

Scene Three

THÉRÈSE, in a red power suit, plays a tug of war with IGNACE Gamelin. They are at the height of their argument.

IGNACE
I tell you Thérèse, productivity at the Ironworks is down! Way down! And the quality of the iron is plummeting with it!

THÉRÈSE
Then perhaps we are trying to accomplish too much in too short a time. If we just focused on producing in smaller volumes we may find that the quality of the iron we do produce is of a higher standard.

IGNACE
It doesn't work like that, Thérèse. We make a little, we make a lot. The problem is the same. Our castings crack!

THÉRÈSE
Maybe it's as simple as too much sand in the mouldings or...

IGNACE
Why do you go on about things you know nothing about and couldn't possibly understand.

THÉRÈSE
Be patient with me, Ignace. I'm just trying to help.

IGNACE
I'm sorry, my dear. But I am running out of patience. And we are running out of time. The bottom line is this. We're losing money. And at the rate we're going, we're not going to make the King's quota. We default on the quota, we lose the king's patronage. We lose Louis' patronage, we lose the Ironworks!

THÉRÈSE
What do you want me to do!?

IGNACE
Sell! Sell your shares in the Ironworks to François Etiennes Cugnet.

THÉRÈSE
I can't, Ignace!

IGNACE
We need him, Thérèse.

THÉRÈSE
I can't, Ignace. I just can't. You need him so badly then why don't you sell.

IGNACE
Because I built this Ironworks! From the ground up! Together with François! And I have invested more than sentimentality. If you loved your husband, you would respect what he was trying to achieve with this enterprise. Instead of trying to destroy it.

THÉRÈSE
I'm not trying to destroy it!

IGNACE
Then sell your shares to Cugnet! And I promise you, you'll be handsomely rewarded.

THÉRÈSE
I can't! I won't!

> *THÉRÈSE appears to be winning.*

IGNACE
Then you will be the ruin of us all!

> *He lets go. THÉRÈSE falls back on her behind. ANGÉLIQUE helps her up.*

Scene Four

> *The kitchen.*

MANON
I've come for the fish.

ANGÉLIQUE
The fish? What fish?

MANON
The fish you made.

ANGÉLIQUE
I don't make the fish. I just cook it.

MANON
Madame de Francheville promised my mistress some fish.

ANGÉLIQUE
Well, if Madame de Francheville promised…. Here.

> *She holds up a fish skeleton but with the head and tail still
> attached.*

It's little thin but it's really tasty. As big as ol' Madame de Beray is,
she doesn't need much more. *(beat)* Kinda looks like her, doesn't it?
Only prettier.

(using the fish head to speak) Eh, Manon. *J'ai faim. Va me chercher un
poisson. Je veux manger du poisson. Je suis un poisson. Je vais me
manger moi meme! (fish wrestling)* Aghhhhh! *(seeing that MANON
is not amused)* Oh, come on. Laugh, Manon. I'm only trying to have
some fun. Life is what it is but we can always share a laugh. Yes?
(when MANON doesn't reply) Well, I guess not.

> *ANGÉLIQUE gives MANON a Corning casserole dish.*

Here. Angélique's famous fish stew. I hope the old bitch doesn't
choke on it.

> *MANON takes it and starts to exit. ANGÉLIQUE stops her.*

ANGÉLIQUE
Manon… I am only trying to be your friend. I know I get lonely
sometimes. Don't you? So far from home. I wish I had a friend, to
make the time go lighter.

MANON
César was my friend! He made me laugh. He spoke my language.

ANGÉLIQUE

I didn't know you felt that way about him.

MANON

He was good to me... until you came. Maybe when you go he will be good again.

ANGÉLIQUE

It was you he.... Oh, Manon. I am so sorry. I didn't know.... Maybe he will make you laugh again. César is free. At least, he's free of me.

MANON

He will never be free of you.

ANGÉLIQUE

But that's not my fault. That wasn't my fault, Manon. You can't blame me...

MANON

When you go... *(exits)*

ANGÉLIQUE

But I'm not going...

Scene Five

THÉRÈSE at her computer.

THÉRÈSE

As of Monday, you'll be staying at the home of my brother-in-law, Alexis Le Moine Moniere.

ANGÉLIQUE

Madame...?

THÉRÈSE

You will stay there until the first canoe leaves for Quebec – where I have made arrangements for you to be sold to Monsieur Cugnet.

ANGÉLIQUE

Sold...

VOICEOVER

(whispered) Angélique... Angélique?

ANGÉLIQUE
Madame…. No…. Madame please… you can't…

THÉRÈSE
I can. And I have.

ANGÉLIQUE
But I belong to Monsieur.

VOICEOVER
(whispered) Angélique… Angélique?

THÉRÈSE
You belong to me. Did you think you were freed by his death?

ANGÉLIQUE
But why, Madame? Why? I thought things were better, Madame.
I thought I was serving you better…. No one ever served you better.

THÉRÈSE
(calmly) I don't want you. I have never wanted you here. And
I welcome the opportunity to be rid of you. You have brought
nothing but unhappiness and misery into my home. You will lie
with anyone. César. My husband. Now Claude. Gamelin is right. You
are like animals. *Vous êtes trop matinée.* I cannot live with that. I have
had no choice but to endure your presence while François lived. But
now that's over.

ANGÉLIQUE
(grovelling at THÉRÈSE's feet) You can't sell me, Madame, please
don't sell me.

VOICEOVER
(whispered) Angélique… Angélique?

ANGÉLIQUE
I can't take another master. I can't. Master after master. Never
knowing which one will be the death of me. I can't go though this
all over again.

THÉRÈSE
It is too late. The arrangements have been made.

ANGÉLIQUE
No! Madame. Please. Please…

THÉRÈSE exits.

Scene Six

Fury.

ANGÉLIQUE
YOU BITCH! I WON'T TAKE ANOTHER MASTER! I'LL KILL
BEFORE I HAVE ANOTHER MASTER! I'LL KILL YOU! I'll strangle
you in your sleep! I'll poison your food! You stingy whore! I'll make
you rue the day you sell me! I'll… I'll…

CLAUDE
Calm down…

ANGÉLIQUE
Take me to New England! Now!

CLAUDE
But that's impossible.

ANGÉLIQUE
You promised me, Claude.

CLAUDE
But we can't just pick up and leave like that.

ANGÉLIQUE
Then I will go alone!

CLAUDE
You'll never make it.

ANGÉLIQUE
I don't care!

CLAUDE
Wait. Listen. *(She struggles with him.)* Listen to me. I'll take you.
I made a promise and I won't break it. But we can't leave now. I have

to plan our escape carefully. Cause we'll only get one stab at it. We get caught we're as good as dead. Until then, just sit tight.

ANGÉLIQUE
How will we know when the is time is right?

CLAUDE
Don't worry. You'll know.

Scene Seven

MANON works outside, singing quietly to herself. ANGÉLIQUE enters and works at her separate tasks. There is some distance between them. There is a large cracking sound.

ANGÉLIQUE
What was that?

MANON
The ice.

CLAUDE
(walking through with a sack of potatoes) It's certainly warming up. *(to ANGÉLIQUE)* Soon. *(He begins to whistle a lively tune.)*

ANGÉLIQUE
(softly, to MANON) When we crossed the great river, some leapt into the water to become froth upon the waves. Some hunkered on their haunches and simply willed themselves to sleep. 'Cause when the spirit leaves the body it flies home to the motherland. What do you see when you look to the river?

MANON does not respond.

What do you hear? *(They look at each other.)* How fast your heart must beat when you look in that direction. Knowing home is close and yet impossible to reach. Does not your spirit yearn to fly this place? Are not your memories still fresh? How do you stop your feet from taking you to where you belong?

MANON
I am where I belong.

THÉRÈSE and IGNACE crossing through the scene.

THÉRÈSE
…six hundred pounds!

IGNACE
For her? *(referring to ANGÉLIQUE)*

THÉRÈSE
Yes. Have I done well in my negotiations?

IGNACE
Not bad.

THÉRÈSE
Perhaps I will be a good entrepreneur after all.

IGNACE
Well, I wouldn't go that far.

THÉRÈSE
(laughing) Oh, Ignace.

> *They exit.*

ANGÉLIQUE
Bitch!

> *MANON laughs.*

You think that's funny? You won't be laughing when the same thing happens to you.

MANON
They say you come from the land of the devil. That the blackness of your skin is the blackness of your soul scorched by the fires of hell.

ANGÉLIQUE
They say that you are bloodthirsty savages. Pagan children, shameless in their nakedness. What does it matter what they say. We are here. Today!

MANON
We are not the same. I serve. I do not slave.

ANGÉLIQUE

A dog and a jackal meet in the forest. "How is it," asks the jackal, that you are so fat and I am so poor and we are both the same animal? The dog says, "I lay around my master's house and let him kick me and he gives me food." "Better then," says the jackal, "that I stay poor."

MANON

Look. Just leave me alone. Okay? Our ways are different. Our stories. Our paths.

ANGÉLIQUE

I'm sorry. I thought I recognized something old and familiar.

MANON

I don't follow you. Do not follow me.

ANGÉLIQUE

I won't. You have forgotten the way.

Scene Eight

All voices in unison: "April 10, 1734."

MANON

(*shovelling hot coals into a bucket*)
My raging heart,
Wey a hey a
Is filled with pain,
Wey a hey a
My César's frost,
Wey a hey a
is searing me,
Wey a hey a.

My blood flows hot,
Wey a hey a
My breath blows cold,
Wey a hey a
Memories of his love,
Wey a hey a
Still burn in me,
Wey a hey.

She ululates. CÉSAR enters with a cigar, matches and cigar scissors. He takes the bucket from MANON and prepares the cigar for smoking.

CÉSAR

I smile. I grin. I keep my eyes averted. I "*Oui*, Monsieur." "*Non*, Monsieur." "Right away, Monsieur." I do whatever I have to do to "just get along." It's survival in the white man's world. And I get by. Why fight what I can't change? But don't think that makes me any less a man.

Don't look at me too closely. You'll see the smile is on my lips not in my eyes which see everything. And though my head is bent, my backbone's strong. My shoulders broad and powerful. And these hands could crush a windpipe just like an autumn leaf. But I don't fight. I'll do whatever I gotta do to "just get along."

Claude thinks that he can beat me with a word. 'Cause in this world where white is might a word is all it takes to silence. But I am a patient man. I'll wait it out. And when the time is right. *(handing the cigar to IGNACE and lighting a match)* I'll strike!

He hands the cigar to IGNACE, who takes a light from CÉSAR. He puffs on the cigar a bit, with satisfaction, before speaking. CÉSAR puts the pail beside him.

IGNACE

Women have no place in business. Their minds can't seem to get around their emotions. And there is no room in business for emotion. I let Thérèse have her way. But she will sell. *(He puffs.)* Eventually, she'll have to sell. *(He flicks his ash into the bucket.)*

THÉRÈSE enters with a candle and slowly makes her way across the stage occasionally stopping and looking behind her, as if she is being pursued by something which isn't there.

THÉRÈSE

(stopping) Who's there? Angélique? *(silence)* There are too many noises in this house. Creeks and bumps. Sounds I can't identify. Hear that? *(She stops, listens, whispers.)* Angélique? *(She continues.)* This is my house! I know this house. I love this house. But everything sounds strange to me. Cats cry each night. Dogs howl. Horses stamp their feet. They sense it too. *(She stops.)* Who's there? Angélique? *(pause) Les Lutins.* Yes. Goblins. They're back. I didn't think they

could stray so far from farms. But yes! *Les Lutins*. That makes sense. *(She relaxes.)* Yes. Goblins. I can deal with goblins. Goblins and Angélique. Both, I can be rid of.

> *She takes the bucket and hands it to CLAUDE, who enters with an oil lamp.*

CLAUDE
I'm going to be somebody someday. You think I'm going to be hauling buckets and shovelling horseshit all my life? Not me. I'll be as big as Francheville one day. Bigger. You see, I am. I am more than... I am more than this!

In New France, I'll never be more than peasant scum who signed five years of his life away for some new clothes, a few bags of grain and a stony piece of land that may never bear fruit. But in New England or farther south, there's no telling what a man could make of himself! Yes. There's money to be made in the colonies. And, you know what...?

> *He puts the bucket down and gives ANGÉLIQUE a passionate kiss.*

I'm going to make me some.

ANGÉLIQUE
Love. I had almost forgotten it felt like... freedom.

CLAUDE
Soon.

> *He exits leaving the pail with ANGÉLIQUE.*

ANGÉLIQUE
How long can I wait? Each minute brings me closer to a living death. And I'm alive. I am alive!

His touches burn, sear, scorch, igniting fire deep inside where pain and ice had been. And I feel... heat, life, force, power, Black and strong.

She envies that. Cold, passionless bitch! Just like her bastard husband. Both sucking. Sucking life. Denying life.

No! I am not a chair, a sack of grain or a calf to be fattened and sold for slaughter! I am alive. And loved. And I can't wait… any longer.

Smoke begins to fill the stage.

THÉRÈSE
Fire!

ANGÉLIQUE
Fire!

IGNACE
Fire!

CÉSAR
Fire!

> *Pandemonium breaks out. Church bells ringing, people shouting, panicking. The actors run around and organize themselves into a line in which buckets pass from person to person. ANGÉLIQUE is at the end of the line. Buckets pass swiftly and desperately from person to person. CLAUDE enters picking his teeth. Watches silently for a moment. ANGÉLIQUE turns to grab another bucket, sees CLAUDE and, instead, grabs CLAUDE's hand.*

ANGÉLIQUE
Now?

CLAUDE
Now!

> *They run. The line continues to battle the flames which mount higher and higher. They turn and speak rapidly.*

ANGÉLIQUE
The fire was set at the St. Paul Street house of her mistress, in the evening of April 10, 1734.

CLAUDE
The flames travelled quickly from one house to another and, later, to L'Hotel Dieu where the neighbours had started to transport their furniture and belongings.

ANGÉLIQUE
The convent and the church were destroyed.

CLAUDE
This was the third time L'Hotel Dieu had been engulfed by flames.

ANGÉLIQUE
By the time the fire died, 46 homes would be consumed.

Scene Nine

Reporting not unlike "Current Affairs." These scenes are a series of sound bites that play over or are intercut with the ensuing scenes of ANGÉLIQUE and CLAUDE.

REPORTER
It's been determined that yesterday's fire was set by the negress slave of the widow de Francheville, who has escaped with a man named Thibault, also working for de Francheville.

Rumour has it that the negress has often threatened her mistress and the city with the setting of a fire, and that on the same day said that neither her mistress nor many more would sleep in their houses that night. The King's Attorney is calling for the arrest of the negress and the said Thibault.

Scene Ten

ANGÉLIQUE and CLAUDE at a barn near Longueuil. The wind whistles.

CLAUDE
This way... quick... get down.

ANGÉLIQUE
Why are we stopping...?

CLAUDE
Here. Stuff these in your bag...

ANGÉLIQUE
Bread...?

CLAUDE
Six loaves. I hid them two days ago when Madame sent me to Longueuil. It's not much but…

ANGÉLIQUE
Two days ago? Which way now?

CLAUDE
That way. Chemin Chambly.

They run off.

Scene Eleven

THÉRÈSE testifies among the ruins.

THÉRÈSE
Thérèse de Couagne. Age 37. I don't know who set the fire in my house. I did not see the negress go upstairs to the attic unless it was between noon and one o'clock when I went to church for the blessed sacrament. Thibault did come to me the night before and asked to be paid for the time he had worked as my farmer. I told him that I sold the negress and that I didn't want him back in my house either. But I cannot, in all honesty, suspect the negress because there were no fires in my chimneys that day.

Scene Twelve

ANGÉLIQUE and CLAUDE off Chemin de Chambly. They are wrapped in a thick black blanket. Covered by darkness. We hear the thundering sound of horses, wooden wheels turning on a rocky road. Throwing the shadow of its spokes on the mound of the blanket, where we see just the faces of ANGÉLIQUE and CLAUDE frozen with fear, panic, desperation. The sound subsides as it moves into the distance. They remain immobile until there is stillness. Then ANGÉLIQUE and CLAUDE slowly emerge out of the darkness into the dim cast of moonlight.

Scene Thirteen

*IGNACE sits comfortably in an arm chair. He is obviously at home
and untouched by the fire. CÉSAR stands by him. He testifies.*

IGNACE
Ignace Gamelin. And I am old enough to be your father!

Slaves are notoriously inefficient and unwilling. A horse – if it is well
treated and cared for, will gladly return all the effort which a well-
loved master demands. Some slaves are like horses in this respect *(He
smiles at CÉSAR.)* But most are not. Their sense of freedom chafes at
restraint. To kindness and forbearance they return insolence and
contempt. Nothing awes or governs them but the whip or the dread
of sale.

It's fascinating…. While kept in subjugation, they are submissive
and easy to control. But let any of them be indulged with the hope
of freedom. Then they reject all restraint and become wholly un-
manageable: as is the case with this heinous act of arson. It is by the
expectation of liberty, and by that alone, that they can be rendered
a threat to the population.

Scene Fourteen

The woods. ANGÉLIQUE sits in frustration.

ANGÉLIQUE
The same. Everything looks the same. Those trees, this rock…. Are
you sure we're not just running around in circles?

CLAUDE
(angry) Look. I know where I am going! Okay?

ANGÉLIQUE
(surprised) Okay, Claude. *(as he stalks off)* Okay. *(She follows.)*

Scene Fifteen

Testimony.

MANON

Manon, Huron. Age, 19. Just hours before the fire, Angélique came over to me and tried to make me laugh. But I wasn't in the mood. She said, "You really don't want to laugh? You see Madame de Francheville there laughing with Monsieur Gamelin? Well, she won't have a house to sleep in." Angélique thought that was funny.

Scene Sixteen

ANGÉLIQUE and CLAUDE in the woods. Cold, dirty, tired.

ANGÉLIQUE

I don't want to take the chance.

CLAUDE

But we're so far away. They have probably stopped looking for us by now.

ANGÉLIQUE

What if they haven't? If we light a fire the smoke will lead them right to us.

CLAUDE

Angélique. It's been days since we've been indoors. We'll freeze to death.

ANGÉLIQUE

(beat) No we won't. Come here.

He goes to her and she wraps herself around him and kisses him.

We're going to make it.

She starts to make love to him.

Scene Seventeen

*The testimonies continue. The following testimonies are doubled by
the remaining cast. These are like the specious and ridiculous eye-
witnesses often seen on many sensational news programs.*

MARGEURITE

Margeurite de Couagne. Age 10. I don't know who set the fire in my
aunt's house but just before the fire Angélique was sulking in the
kitchen and then I saw her leave by the door on the street and go talk
to Mr. de Beray's Indian, Manon. Since then I have heard say that the
negress said to the *panisse* that neither she nor her master would
sleep in their house. That's all I know, except that two or three times
before the fire, the man named Thibault was with the negress in
Madame de Franchevilles' kitchen.

HYPOLITE

Hypolite Lebert, esquire. Age 15. I don't know who set the fire in
Madame de Francheville's house. But I heard Monsieur de Beray's
Indian say to Madame de Francheville that her negress said to her
that Mrs. de Francheville would not sleep in her house.

JEANNE

Jeanne Taillandier de la Baume. Age 41. I can't positively say that the
fire was started by the negress but when it started I thought for sure
it was the negress who started it. I have heard from some children
that the negress was threatening to burn her mistress and strangle
her and that the negress has said that if she could go back to her
country and there were Frenchmen there – she would make them all
perish.

The testimonies begin to overlap.

MARIE

Marie Louise Poirier. Age 25. I cannot say anything about the fire but
I have heard that the negress said that if she ever returned to her
country and there were white people there she would burn them like
dogs. That we were worthless. I also know for a fact that the negress
stole three deerskins from Madame de Francheville.

JEAN

Jean Joseph Boudard – 41. All I know are the rumours I've heard
that it was the wicked negress of Madame de Francheville who set
the fire. But sometimes I would see her drinking *Eau de Vie...*

FRANÇOIS
François de Beray. All I know is what Manon told me. That a short time before the fire, the negress told her that her mistress would not sleep in her house…

The REPORTER cutting though the cacophony.

REPORTER
In dramatic new developments in the O. J.—I mean M. J. Angélique—case, four-year-old Amable Le Moine was brought before the court. Amable, daughter of Alexis Le Moine Moniere and brother-in-law of Madame de Francheville, who swore under oath to tell the truth, testified that on the day of the fire she saw the negress, Marie Joseph Angélique, carrying a coal shuttle up to the attic.

Scene Eighteen

Black. The sound of two wild animals fighting. In the ensuing silence we hear…

CLAUDE
I'm afraid.

Scene Nineteen

CLAUDE and ANGÉLIQUE, wet, ragged, dirty, tired, in the woods.

CLAUDE
If we don't find food, we'll starve to death.

ANGÉLIQUE
We'll be in New England soon. It's been almost two weeks.

CLAUDE
I don't know. I don't know. I was thinking. We passed a cabin a little while back…

ANGÉLIQUE
That was days ago…

CLAUDE
There could be food... warmth...

ANGÉLIQUE
You want to go back?

CLAUDE
Go back...?

ANGÉLIQUE
We can never go back.

CLAUDE
Not after what's happened. Not after...

ANGÉLIQUE
What?

CLAUDE
You know. The fire.

ANGÉLIQUE
What's that got to do with us?

CLAUDE
It doesn't matter now.

ANGÉLIQUE
Claude, you didn't start that fire? Did you?

CLAUDE
(regards her for a long moment) No.

ANGÉLIQUE
Then what do we care! Let's just try to leave it all behind. *(trying to raise his spirits)* It's hard. I know. Sometimes I doubt we're ever going to make it. But we've come this far. We're still alive. And close. New England feels so close. If we can just keep pushing forward...

CLAUDE
Angélique...?

ANGÉLIQUE
Yes...

CLAUDE

…you're right. *(pulling her closer to him)* And when we get to New England, we'll dine on pheasant and roasted potatoes and wash it all down with tankards of beer…

ANGÉLIQUE

Stop. Stop. You're making it worse.

CLAUDE

I know. My stomach is cramping at the thought.

ANGÉLIQUE

Will they have ships there?

CLAUDE

Maybe…

ANGÉLIQUE

Then I will take you home. You will like my land. It's warmer there. And always green. And food hangs from the trees.

CLAUDE

Just like the Garden of Eden.

ANGÉLIQUE

You will see. You'll see.

She curls up against him and sleeps.

Scene Twenty

ANGÉLIQUE sleeps.

CLAUDE

I remember watching my mother's back – always bent, her shirt sleeves rolled above the wrinkles on her elbows. The skin on her arms and hands – rough and red and flaky. She scrubbed laundry for the rich… for pennies. Some days I would beg more than she earned.

And I promised myself that before I left this miserable world, I would become something more than just another hungry peasant or a common petty thief.

So I jumped at the chance to come to this new world. There are opportunities here that I can't even begin to imagine. Just sitting there waiting to be discovered.

I've done everything for you. I've burnt... I've burnt down my dreams for you. But with you, I'll always be running. And I can't run anymore. I can't. I'm sorry. I just can't do it. Please... understand. I can't. I can't. I can't.

He runs off.

Scene Twenty-One

ANGÉLIQUE wakes up alone in the woods to the lonely whistling of the wind through the trees.

ANGÉLIQUE
Claude... Claude...? I had a dream. Claude? We were in New England. But it wasn't New England. It was my village, Claude. Home! I was home. And the sun was setting below the water just as the fire was rising. And you were there. Claude? That's a good sign.... Yes? Claude? *(pause)* Where are you? *(pause)* Claude, are you there? *(silence)* Claaaude!

No response. ANGÉLIQUE listens. Searches for him in all directions with the growing realization that she is alone in the woods. Somewhere, she doesn't know where. Abandoned. No food. No idea of what direction she should follow. She sits, refusing to cry.

It was a good sign. Claude. We could have made it.

Scene Twenty-Two

The lights slowly fall and rise like the setting and the dawning of the sun. ANGÉLIQUE sits in the same place staring out into space. She begins to softly sing a long forgotten song of her home land – accompanied by the muted beating of a drum. Over the course of this speech, two men come and drag her off. She does not resist. The speech continues on an empty stage.

VOICEOVER

Marie Joseph Angélique is declared guilty of setting the fire to
Madame de Franchevilles' house, which proceeded to burn down the
city. For redress of the damages caused by the fire, and other facts
mentioned at the trial, will she make public amends by wearing a
shirt only, with a noose around her neck, holding in her hands a
burning torch weighing two pounds, in front of the main door and
entrance of the parish church of this city, where she will be taken by
the executioner of the high court in a tip cart used to pick up
garbage and wearing a sign inscribed with the word "arsonist" on her
front and back. There, on her knees, will she declare in a loud and
clear voice that she wickedly and ill-advisedly set the fire, for which
she repents and asks God, the King, and justice for forgiveness.
This done, she will be taken to the public place of the said city of
Montreal, to be hanged and strangled to death from the gallows
erected for that purpose, her body burned at the stake, the ashes
scattered to the wind and her belongings seized in the name of the
King. Prior, the accused will be tortured in both the ordinary and
extraordinary means to reveal the identity of her accomplices and
concerning the said Thibault.

Scene Twenty-Three

*FRANÇOIS enters dressed in neutral modern clothes and reads
from a book.*

FRANÇOIS

Monday, June 21, 1734. 7am. The accused had her shoes taken off
and was put on the torture seat by the torturer, and after she'd been
strapped in the usual manner with the buskins tied, the accused
said...

*During this CLAUDE enters dressed in the same fashion, as do all
the actors.*

CLAUDE

She has no knowledge of anyone and that it's not her. She said "no
one helped her because she didn't set the fire."

FRANÇOIS

After the wedge was tightened she said I want to die...

CÉSAR enters.

CÉSAR
At the second blow, she said I'd rather die. No one set, or has helped me set the fire.

MANON enters.

MANON
At the third blow, she said the same.

THÉRÈSE enters.

THÉRÈSE
At the fourth blow she said to hang her, that it was her alone.

IGNACE enters.

IGNACE
After that, for the extraordinary torture, we had a second wedge put in and hit... and hit... and hit... and hit...

FRANÇOIS
She said...

CÉSAR
Kill me.

MANON
It's me alone.

THÉRÈSE
Hang me. It's me.

ANGÉLIQUE enters. She is barefoot and naked under a rough raw cotton period shirt.

THIBAULT
It's me with a hot plate. No one did it with me.

ANGÉLIQUE
No one helped me, nor suggested it. It was my own initiative.

She takes the book.

It's me, Monsieurs. Let me die.

She closes the book.

Scene Twenty-Four

ANGÉLIQUE steps up to a microphone.

ANGÉLIQUE
My name is Marie Josephe Angélique.
I am twenty-nine years old.
I came from Portugal, from the island of Madiere
where I was sold to a Flemish,
who brought me to this New World
and sold me to Monsieur de Francheville.
But before...
before...

Look!
The view is clear...
So clear from here.
In the vista of tomorrow
stretching out before,
I can see this city...
swarming with ebony.
There's me and me and me and me...
My brothers and my sisters!

My brothers and my sisters...
Arrested for their difference.
Their misery
a silent scream,
rising to crescendo
and
falling on deaf ears.

There is nothing I can say to change what you perceive.
I will from twisted history,
be guilty in your eyes.
If thought is sin
then I am guilty.
For I wish that I had fanned the flames that lead to your destruction.
But though I am wretched,
I am not wicked.

Almost ecstatic.

Take my breath.
Burn my body.
Throw my ashes to the wind.
Set my spirit free.
The truth cannot be silenced.
Someday,
someone will hear me
and believe...
I didn't do it.

Until then...

Drums start beating softly and grow.

I am going home.

The hangman goes to put the noose around her neck. She takes it from him.

Can you see the fires rise to greet the sunset?

She puts the noose around her own neck. A male voice calls softly from the crowd.

CLAUDE
(whispers) Angélique. Angélique.

The soft sound of drums building.

ANGÉLIQUE
Do you hear it? Drums!

The sound of the platform giving way beneath her. Her silhouetted figure dancing on wall. The overpowering sound of drums. Black.

The end.

Born in Montreal, Lorena was an award-winning actress, director and writer. *Je me souviens*, her second play, was a finalist for the Governor General's Literary Award in 2002, received three Jessie Richardson Award nominations (2000) and was selected by the *Vancouver Sun* as one of the Ten Best Plays of 2000. Her first play, *Angélique*, had its American premiere at the Detroit Repertory Theatre and in New York, off-Broadway at Manhattan Class Company Theatre, where it was nominated for eight Audelco Awards (New York Black Theatre Awards). *Angélique* premiered at Alberta Theatre Projects Pan Canadian playRites Festival '98 and was nominated Outstanding New Play in Calgary's Betty Mitchell Awards. Lorena published articles in *Canadian Theatre Review*, *CanPlay*, and her personal essay, "Where Beauty Sits," was published in the anthology *But Where Are You Really From* by Sister Vision Press. Lorena passed away in July 2009.